EAST SUS WALK

C000000854

2. IN AND AROUND THE RURAL VILLAGES

Sandy Hernu

S.B. Publications

For my brother, Jeremy

First published in 1994 by S.B. Publications
c/o 19 Grove Road, Seaford, East Sussex BN25 1TP

© Copyright 1994 Sandy Hernu

All rights reserved. No part of this publication may be reprinted, reproduced or utilized in any form or by any electronic, mechanical or other means, now known or hereafter invented, including photocopying and recording, or in any information storage or retrieval system, without the permission of both the copyright holder and the publisher of this book.

ISBN 1 85770 059 7

Typeset and printed by Island Press Ltd, 0323 490222 UK

CONTENTS

	page
The Author	4
Introduction	5
Map showing location of walks	8
Key to Maps	9
1. Winchelsea	10
2. Burwash to Batemans	16
3. Pevensey and Westham	22
4. Ditchling and The Lanes	28
5. Alfriston	33
6. Rushlake Green and Warbleton	39
7. Fairlight	45
8. Waldron	50
9. Hartfield to Withyham	54
10. Northiam and Great Dixter	61
11. Berwick and Alciston	67
12. Southease and Rodmell	73
13. Mayfield	78
14. Sedlescombe	85
15. Around Fletching	90
The Country Code	95
Transport and Tourist Information Centres	96

Front Cover: *Fletching*
Back Cover: *Pevensey Castle*
Title Page: *Westham*

This verse, engraved on an early nineteenth century mug, surely sums up a farmer's view of rural life at that time. Who it is written by, I do not know, otherwise I would gladly acknowledge him or her. However, it seemed appropriate to include it in this book.

Let the wealthy and great
Roll in splendour and state
I envy them not, I declare it
I eat my own lamb
My own chickens and ham
I shear my own fleece and I wear it

I have lawns, I have bowers
I have fruits, I have flowers
The lark is my morning alarmer
So jolly boys now
Here's God speed to the plough
Long life and success to the
Farmer

THE AUTHOR

Brought up and having lived in Sussex for many years, Sandy Hernu shares her love of both, the countryside and history, by writing the second in a short series of books about Sussex.

Sandy and her husband, Jeffrey, live in Alfriston, Sussex.

By the same author:-
Exploring Alfriston and the Cuckmere Valley (1992)
East Sussex Walks: Brighton, Eastbourne and Lewes area (1993)

INTRODUCTION

This is the second book of the East Sussex Walks series, bringing together the often hidden aspects of local landscapes with a little of its heritage and main points of interest. At a recent talk, I was asked where and what did my interest of both the countryside and history stem from.

I suppose, on reflection, the countryside bit began when I was seven years old. My elder brother, who was then working on a nearby farm, would come home with all sorts of rural tales to tell. I used to pester him and continually ask for yet more stories about the farm and I think, certainly initially, just to keep this brat of a sister quiet, he decided we would walk there and he'd show it to me instead. How he must have regretted that decision, because thereafter, the minute he stepped through the door hoping for a peaceful weekend, I nagged him to take me for one of his "special walks". It was all such fun and interesting too.

He showed me where the speckled thrushes nested, the difference between rabbits and long eared hares. Where the early wild primroses grew and the unusual Bee Orchid, which hid in sheltered corners of the Downs. Where to find red berried holly that nobody else knew about or the first tiny mushrooms of Autumn. Sometimes we would feed the perpetually muddy farm horse, a feat in itself, as one would have to keep out of the way of a particularly vicious donkey at the same time. We watched the farmer ploughing long straight furrows and one day, in the adjacent woods found a badger's set. After frequent visits we were rewarded with old "brock" venturing forth, then shuffling off with an ungainly plod.

My brother's "piece de resistance" for his little sister (repeated many times, for at that age I thought it was the funniest thing ever) was to lie down in a field full of cows and wait, whilst they eyed him with curiosity. Sure enough, little by little, they would edge closer, sheer nosiness overcoming any wariness they might feel until finally, the entire herd would be sniffing at his boots or thrusting soft noses and rough tongues into his side, whilst he stroked them. To this day, I can never resist a few minutes "chat" to these exceedingly inquisitive and very gentle creatures.

As I got older, my tastes became a little more sophisticated and I went for many walks throughout Sussex with my parents, visiting villages "en route". My father, a source of information on local history, would impart his knowledge about each area, coupled with its legends and traditions. He made it easy to imagine smugglers creeping through the water-logged marshes of Pett, the splendid King Alfred hunting at Ditchling or the sounds of the Wealden iron industry echoing through the valleys and villages of Burwash, Waldron, Hellingly, Mayfield and the like. I loved the story about the eccentric M.P., known as Mad Jack Fuller of Brightling, who built various follies and as he requested upon his death, buried in his mausoleum, wearing not much more than a top hat.

It haunted me that vagrancy could have been such a terrible crime that the offenders were publicly whipped, or that Richard Woodman, called the Iron Man, had to be burnt at the stake in Lewes simply because of his religious beliefs. I envisaged stepping back in the past just to see how this southerly coastline once looked at the time when the sea encroached as far back as Hailsham, crept over the flats of Pevensey, surrounded Winchelsea and covered the entirety of Romney Marsh.

I look back on those early history lessons, for I don't know what else to call them, rather wistfully. It seems that what could be left to the imagination then, is really much more exciting than the answers research often produce today. However, fact-finding does suggest that village life was more eventful a hundred years ago. It really has changed dramatically in that comparatively short period of time. Gone are the days when each community was self sufficient, with its own blacksmith, wheelwright, saddler, butcher, grocer, brewer and often a fellmonger, tanner and dressmaker. There was nearly always a village school. Sometimes, when walking through the surrounding woods and hills, it is easy to see how several small fields have been amalgamated to make one large field, traces of the divisory walls or hedges still in evidence. Now there is usually one large farm instead of three and one farm worker to the six needed in the last century.

The villagers themselves were mostly poor. Families of seven or eight would be crowded together in two rooms, with mother still having to take in washing and ironing to make ends meet. Daughters would hopefully find work as servants at the local manor, sons toiled on the farms from dawn to dusk. How the twentieth century has altered all this and so quickly too. The traders referred to have almost disappeared, their premises converted to comfortable homes, frequently with only a name as a reminder of the past and all too often, inhabitants seem to guard their preserved villages with undue zeal, anxious lest a stray tourist should spoil the peace and quiet. Do they forget that in the past, their little hamlet was a hive of activity?

Walking through the highways, byways and villages of this perenially beautiful part of the country, I was struck by the many varied aspects it has to offer. There is everything the visitor, sightseer, walker or hiker could wish for. The undulating sheer white cliffs, aptly called The Seven Sisters, running from Cuckmere Haven to Eastbourne, with the glorious Downs as a backdrop, stretching for nearly seventy miles and the average breadth being seven miles, provide some of the best scenery in England. There are the colourful woodlands of the High Weald, the purple heathlands of Ashdown Forest or the salty green marshland surrounding Pevensey, Winchelsea and Rye. From tiny flint cottages to huge castles bearing the Norman influence, it's there just waiting for us to enjoy it.

All of the walks in this book, circular except for one, encapsulate the features mentioned. The terrain on the whole is fairly easy and any road trekking is along country lanes only. The villages are scattered throughout the county, thus enabling everybody to become aquainted with the atmosphere, characteristics and charm that belongs to East Sussex.

EAST SUSSEX

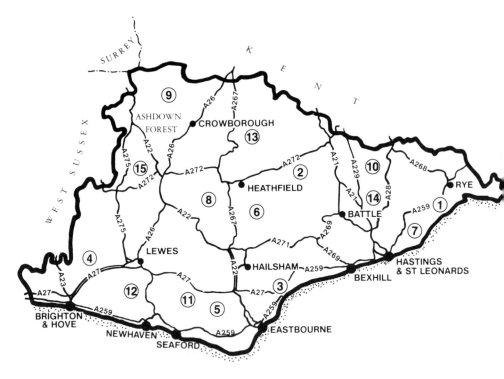

LOCATION OF WALKS

1. Winchelsea
2. Burwash to Batemans
3. Pevensey and Westham
4. Ditchling and The Lanes
5. Alfriston
6. Rushlake Green and Warbleton
7. Fairlight
8. Waldron
9. Hartfield to Withyham
10. Northiam and Great Dixter
11. Berwick and Alciston
12. Southease and Rodmell
13. Mayfield
14. Sedlescombe
15. Around Fletching

KEY TO MAPS

1. Maps are not to scale.

2. All Points of Interest are underlined on the maps.

3. All numbers on the maps indicate Route Directions (see text as well).

4. ℗ denotes a Parking Place.

5. Railways are marked by a crossed line.

Walk 1

WINCHELSEA

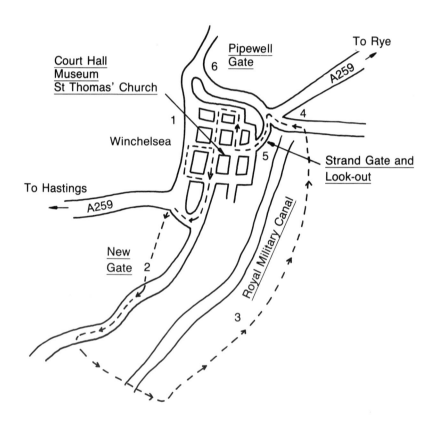

1. Winchelsea
2. New Gate
3. Royal Military Canal
4. Strand Bridge
5. Strand Gate
6. Pipewell Gate

Walk 1

WINCHELSEA

Distance	Approx. 3 miles.
Route	Winchelsea — New Gate — Royal Military Canal — Strand Bridge — Strand Gate — Pipewell Gate — Winchelsea.
Maps	O/S Pathfinder 1291.
Start/Parking	In village centre, just off the A259, Hastings to Rye road.
Public Transport	Hastings to Folkestone buses 11 & 12.
Refreshments	The New Inn, Winchelsea.

The town of Old Winchelsea lies buried on the flat shoreland, somewhere between Camber Sands, southeast of Rye and Fairlight. Its exact site is still uncertain. In the 12th century it was a thriving town, a prosperous port and shipbuilding centre, much larger than the neighbouring Rye. But its vulnerability to violent coastal storms, coupled with unusually high tides and erosion in the latter half of the 13th century led to its demise. It was after one particularly devastating storm, when the sea attacked with greater force than ever before and washed across the buildings, some of which were already derelict, that Old Winchelsea was destroyed for ever.

The loss of this important trading port was brought to the attention of Edward I and national funds were lent to rebuild a bigger and better Winchelsea on the safe site of the nearby Iham Hill. Inhabitants were given roughly the same size plots of land as the ones they had lost. Public buildings were erected and wine cellars built to house the wine imported from France. To the north, where the sea was deep, lay a sheltered harbour and finally, on the hilltop, commanding splendid views, stood the magnificent St. Thomas' Church. The planning was carefully done and laid out in an almost French boulevard fashion, with wide streets and gates at each entrance to the town.

Sadly, New Winchelsea was not to enjoy its wealth and importance for long. By the 15th century it had suffered from the plague and seven dreadful invasions from France. Homes and churches were pillaged then destroyed. People were killed or fled in terror and to add to this dramatic decline the port began to silt up. So as the sea retreated once more from Winchelsea, so did the wealthy traders, the ships, the hustle and bustle and the splendour.

Nevertheless, over the years the chequered history, church and buildings have been preserved. Although the town is much smaller now, the wide streets and squares are almost identical to those laid out six hundred years ago. The town gates, or what remains of them still stand like sentinels gurading their little windswept town on Iham Hill.

I think as one does this walk around the peaceful and lovely Winchelsea, it is essential to pause for a few moments at the look-out by Strand Gate. Here the feeling of this town's turbulent past is all embracing. Certainly as one gazes across the old Military Canal and silent marshes to the sea and France, you realise just how different it is from anywhere else.

Royal Military Canal

Route Directions

This walk starts at the kissing gates at the corner of the churchyard in Winchelsea (1). Keeping the church on the left and the New Inn on the right, continue along the road which will eventually bear right past a walled field. Now turn sharp left down a narrow footpath. Turn right when reaching another road and pass under New Gate (2). The Town Ditch is on the right and Wickham Manor on the hill ahead. Turn left at the next gate and stile, go through the field and gateway opposite, then cross a concrete bridge, this spans the disused Royal Military Canal (3). Follow the path along the canal banks for a mile and at the road turn left across Strand Bridge (4). Turn left and left again to ascend Iham Hill. The road goes beneath Strand Gate (5) before turning right, back into Winchelsea.

At this point there is a special "look-out" where, on a clear day, it is possible to see France. Continue past the Post Office and turn right, the old village pump is sited just on the right, by a large handsome property. At the end of the road turn left, in front of you is Pipewell Gate (6) and to the right a splendid view of Rye, built on a hill and capped with a church. Take the next left, turn right by the New Inn and left at the end of the road, past the Wesleyian Chapel. Now go left and left again back past Winchelsea Church.

Points of Interest

The Town Gates

Winchelsea was once a peninsula and the main access points were via the three town gates. New Gate, which possibly had a drawbridge at one time, is where the invading French are supposed to have entered the town. Strand Gate, the oldest, gave entry to the port and Pipewell or Land Gate, provided the only road link to Rye.

Royal Military Canal

During the early part of the 19th century, at the time of the Napoleonic Wars, hundreds of soldiers were stationed along the coast as, yet again, there was the threat of an invasion from France. The canal was constructed at this time to establish a connection from Pett to Hythe. Now its traffic consists of herons, swans and moorhens, with a patient fisherman or two, sitting hopefully with a line on the reeded banks.

The Look-Out

From here the extensive views, so necessary in Winchelsea's war torn years with France, simply offer a wonderful panorama for the spectator to enjoy. To the east you can see Romney Marsh, Lydd, Dungeness Lighthouse and Rye. To the west are the cliffs of Fairlight and Hastings. Ahead sit the green marshes of Pett, the English Channel and, on a clear day, a glimpse of the French coast and the port of Boulogne.

The Court Hall and Museum

This is one of the oldest buildings in Winchelsea, dating from the 14th century or earlier. It is thought to have been considerably altered, so exact dating can be difficult. The ground floor was the gaol and has been used for many years for the mayoral elections at Easter. The upper part houses the museum and has some fascinating local exhibits. It is open to visitors in the summer months.

The Court Hall and Museum, Winchelsea

St Thomas' Church

A visit to this magnificent church should definitely not be missed. It is so simple and light, with a warm stone interior and the most beautiful stained glass. It has been honoured by royal visitors, Queen Mary, then George VI and Queen Elizabeth (who were then The Duke and Duchess of York) and Queen Elizabeth the Queen Mother visited yet again, some years later. Originally, the church had been built in a cruciform but much of it was destroyed during the French raids and it subsequently fell more and more into disrepair. Restoration work did not start until about 1850. On sale inside is a first class history of the church and several informative books about Winchelsea.

St Thomas' Church, Winchelsea.

Walk 2

BURWASH TO BATEMANS

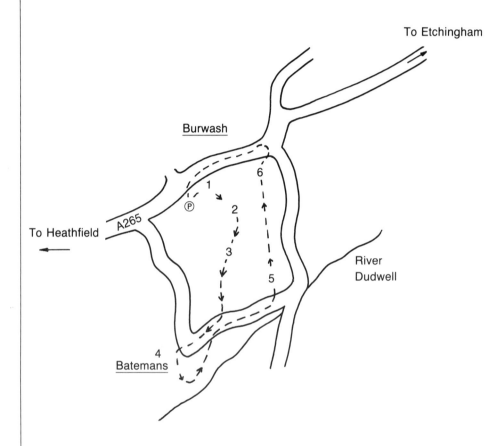

To Etchingham

Burwash

To Heathfield

A265

River
Dudwell

Batemans

1
2
3
4
5
6

1. **Burwash**
2. **Dudwell Valley**
3. **Sussex Squeeze Gate**
4. **Batemans**
5. **Dudwell Farm**
6. **White Cottage**

Walk 2

BURWASH TO BATEMANS

Distance	Approx. 2¼ miles.
Route	Burwash — Dudwell Valley — Sussex Squeeze Gate — Batemans — Dudwell Farm — White Cottage — Burwash.
Maps	O/S Pathfinder 1270.
Start/Parking	On entering Burwash from Heathfield on the A265, turn right into the Public Car Park by the Motel.
Public Transport	Local Rider 318, Heathfield to Hurst Green.
Refreshments	There are several inns, restaurants and teashops in Burwash.

The mellow village of Burwash overlooks the lovely Dudwell Valley to Brightling Beacon beyond. The beacon is the highest point of this particular range of downland and its crowning glory is the 40ft needle, erected by the eccentric Jack Fuller as a result of a wager.

This area now attracts many visitors, not only because of its outstanding natural beauty but because it was adopted by the poet and author, Rudyard Kipling. It was here that he chose to settle from 1902, until his death in 1936, at Batemans, a large stone property, originally built for a prosperous ironmaster, in the 17th century. The house sits comfortably in the folds of the hilly countryside by the Dudwell River and as one descends from Burwash, through woods and fields, one can appreciate why Kipling was ecstatic about his home.

This walk was done at the end of September, with visiting friends. We found the sun dappling russet-edged trees, the hedgerows were hung with blackberries and the terra-cotta tiles of the village were bathed in a soft light that only autumn can provide. It was easy to linger here and suddenly the greater part of the day had passed, delightfully but far too quickly.

Route Directions

Take the footpath by the scout hut, in the corner of the car park at Burwash (1) and cross the stile. Pause for a moment or two to appreciate the extensive views over the Dudwell valley (2). Now go down the hill and bear right over another stile. Cross the next field and stile, then follow the path, keeping the line of oak trees to the right and bearing right through a "Sussex Squeeze" gate (3). Now pass a copse on the right and carry on until reaching a further stile between two gates. Go down the bridleway beyond and turn right for Batemans (4), having reached the road. This handsome house can now be seen nestling in the valley.

On leaving Batemans, return up the road continuing as far as Dudwell Farm (5) and turning left just before the farm buildings. The path here tends to be rather overgrown. Cross a stile and keeping the fence, farm buildings and scrub to the right, proceed for about a hundred yards, turning right over a footbridge and stile. Continue up the hill, with the hedge immediately to the left and at the far end cross the stile leading into woodland. This stile is extremely well hidden, so look for it carefully. At this point the track can become muddy. Cross the next stile and carry on until reaching the White Cottage (6) at the top of the hill. The short path beside it, leads back into Burwash. Turn right to visit the church before returning down the high street to the car park.

Points of interest

Burwash

A picturesque tree-lined village, once the flourishing centre of the Wealden iron industry and where villagers were known as "burrishers". It is well preserved and like others, caters for the visitors, who will find quaint shops to browse in, pubs peppered with history to dine in, a church dating back to Norman times to visit and a number of period houses lining the wide street to look at. The war memorial commands a prominent position, overlooking the church. Amongst others, the name John Kipling catches

The War Memorial, Burwash.

the eye. He was Rudyard Kipling's son, killed at the Battle of Loos in 1915, aged eighteen years.

During the latter part of the eighteenth century, smuggling became rife in Burwash, apparently due to the fact that it lay in a direct line of communication with the coastal village of Pevensey. The Bell Inn, the church and Batemans were favourite haunts for smugglers, not only as meeting places but somewhere to hide their illegal goods. Perhaps it was these legends that inspired Kipling to write 'The Smuggler's Song':

> *Four and twenty ponies, trotting through the dark,*
> *Brandy for the parson, baccy for the clerk,*
> *Them that asks no questions, isn't told a lie,*
> *Watch the wall my darling, whilst the gentlemen go by.*

Batemans

Lying about one mile to the south of Burwash, Batemans is an impressive 17th century house, built of local sandstone with mullioned windows and brick chimneys. Not a great deal is known about its early history, although it is generally presumed it was built for an ironmaster.

Batemans.

Rudyard Kipling purchased the property in 1902 and carried out considerable restoration work. However, there were no major structural alterations, therefore it still retains all its original features.

After Kipling died, in 1936, his wife continued to live at Batemans until her death, three years later. It was Mrs. Kipling who left the entire estate to The National Trust as a memorial to her husband.

The house, gardens, oast houses and mill are open to the public throughout the season.

Burwash High Street.

Walk 3

PEVENSEY AND WESTHAM

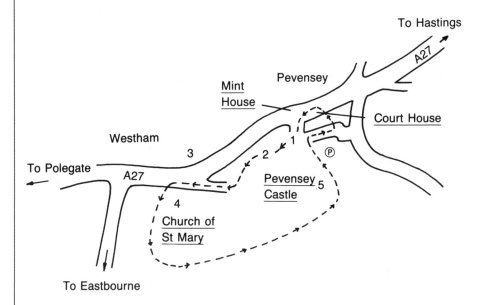

1. **Pevensey**
2. **Pevensey Castle**
3. **Westham**
4. **Church of St Mary**
5. **Anderida**

Walk 3

PEVENSEY AND WESTHAM

Distance	Approx. 1½ miles.
Route	Pevensey — Pevensey Castle — Westham — St. Mary's Church — Anderida — Pevensey.
Maps	O/S Pathfinder 1309.
Start/Parking	At the Car Park in Pevensey on the eastern side of Pevensey Castle.
Public Transport	28 Eastbourne to Rye. 99 Eastbourne to Hastings. British Rail to Westham.
Refreshments	The Pevensey Castle, Westham. Priory Court, The Royal Oak and Castle and The Smugglers at Pevensey.

The walk between Pevensey and Westham is not a long one, but it covers one of the most importantly placed stretches of coastline in our history. In Roman times it acted as a harbour and stronghold against the Saxons and it was near here that William the Conqueror landed on that well known date of 1066, marking the beginning of the Norman invasion of England.

The Roman fort of Anderida, frequently referred to as the outer walls of Pevensey Castle, was built around 340 AD.

At that time Pevensey was a peninsula, the inlet of the sea extending as far back as Hailsham. Part of this walk crosses the marshland at the foot of Anderida, where the sea once broke against the irregular fort walls and boats juddered at their moorings. It is easy to let the imagination run riot, when wandering here or in the castle precincts. Especially when a mist creeps inland, nudging the castle turrets and the damp silence makes you look over your shoulder and wonder if it was a spirit from a bygone era that brushed fleetingly past. Was that noise the stealthy step of a smuggler? Happily it is only imagination, although it could have been fact during the 17th century, when smuggling provided the local inhabitants with a very profitable sideline.

Within a little more than a mile, Pevensey and Westham can offer the visitor, a Roman fort, a Norman castle, 15th century buildings, two churches, one of them being Norman, a 14th century mint house and an old Court House and Gaol. What more can you ask for?

Route Directions

From the car park at Pevensey (1), enter the castle grounds by the eastern arch, opposite The Royal Oak and Castle Inn. Go through the gate and follow the path by the side of the moat and Pevensey Castle (2). Then continue across the precincts to the gate on the western edge, leading into Westham (3). Pass through the gate, into the lane beyond and carry on until reaching the Norman church of St. Mary's (4). Turn left into the churchyard through the Sussex squeeze gate. However, before you do this walk on a little further to look at Westham high street, the Oak House and the old Dial House, both 15th century.

Now return to the churchyard, proceed by the side of the church keeping the hedge to the left at the end, then right, cross the footbridge in the far corner of the graveyard and turn left. Keeping to the left continue across the area of marshland and from here are some splendid views of Anderida (5), the Roman fort. Cross a blue footbridge, turn left and go through the gate ahead, which leads into Pevensey car park. Now turn right down the lane that runs between the two parking areas, turn left opposite St. Nicholas Church and follow the sign to the Court House and Gaol. Turn left by the Court house, back into Pevensey, noting Banks Lodge with an interesting cobbled facia and the Old Mint House, opposite the car park.

Points of Interest

Pevensey Castle

At the Norman Conquest, Pevensey was granted to William the Conqueror's half-brother, The Count of Mortain. It was he, who established the village of Pevensey outside the old Roman fort of Anderida and erected the fortified castle within the already crumbling walls. Substantial repairs had to be made to these, which by then were seven hundred years old. The Castle itself was altered or added to, over the next three hundred years. It was beseiged no less than four times and fell into the possession of various notable families. This probably partially depended on who had found favour with the King. Access to the Roman fort is possible throughout the year, owing to the public footpath that runs through the grounds. The castle is open from March until October.

Entrance to Pevensey Castle.

The Church of St. Mary, Westham

This claims to be the first church the Normans built after landing at Pevensey in 1066. Possibly there was a Saxon church, prior to this date. If so, it was demolished by the Normans, which they did with so many churches, in order to rebuild their own bigger and better edifice. Part of the Norman structure remains today, the rest stems from different eras, including a massive 15th century font, constructed from local greenstone.

The Court House and Gaol

Pevensey Court House is now a museum. The building dates from the latter part of the 16th century, although a Court House has stood on this site since 1207. It consists of a court room, a robing room, two cells and a tiny excercise yard. It was the smallest Town Hall in England and today contains many interesting exhibits and maps.

The Mint House

This intriguing half timbered house, standing in the shadows of the castle, is over six hundred years old. It is built on the site of a Norman Mint, that was in use from 1076 until 1154. Some examples of the coins struck here are in the British Museum. The present house was considerably altered in 1542, when Dr. Andrew Borde, Physician to King Henry VIII lived in it. There are eighteen rooms to see including one, which is panelled with oak carvings from the Renaissance period and another, which is apparently haunted.

The Old Mint House, Pevensey

Walk 4

DITCHLING AND THE LANES

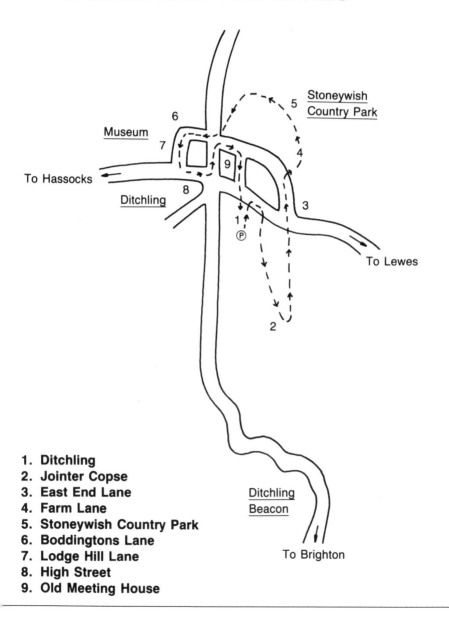

1. Ditchling
2. Jointer Copse
3. East End Lane
4. Farm Lane
5. Stoneywish Country Park
6. Boddingtons Lane
7. Lodge Hill Lane
8. High Street
9. Old Meeting House

Walk 4

DITCHLING AND THE LANES

Distance   Approx. 2 miles.

Route   Ditchling — Jointer Copse — East End Lane —
                        Farm Lane — Stoneywish Country Park —
                        Boddington's Lane — Lodge Hill Lane — High
                        Street — Old Meeting House — Ditchling.

Maps   O/S Pathfinder 1288.

Start/Parking   The car park behind the Village Hall on the B2116,
                        just by Ditchling cross roads.

Public Transport   124, Burgess Hill to Lewes.
                        134, Local Rider to Brighton.

Refreshments   There are several pubs, teashops and restaurants in
                        the village.

This village, below the northern escarpment of the Downs, has charm, historical interest and rural splendour. It is therefore not suprising that Ditchling has attracted artists, writers and celebrities throughout the years. Its proximity to the London-Brighton railway station at nearby Hassocks has made it easily accessible for those who have to work in London.

A well known Ditchling resident is Dame Vera Lynn. The legendary Ellen Terry was once a frequent visitor. The sculptor, Eric Gill and the artist Frank Brangwyn both lived and worked here. Probably the most famous personality of all was Alfred The Great. Evidence suggests he kept a stud of horses and had a hunting park in the Ditchling area.

The route today touches the woodland at the foot of the Downs, where those very hunts took place. From this point you will find superb views of Ditchling Beacon and the Jack and Jill windmills, perched on the skyline at Clayton. Before seeing the Tudor architecture and the fascinating shops and galleries of the village centre, the walk takes in the immediate and very attractive lanes that surround it. Here, the old blends with the new, the pretty gardens are filled with geraniums, roses and flowering shrubs, songbirds constantly warble and footpaths bordered with wildflowers, criss-cross in a rabbit warren fashion. This too, is Ditchling.

The Wagon Shed, Village Green and St. Margarets Church.

Route Directions

From the car park behind the Village Hall at Ditchling (1), turn right and right again by a white house. Follow the footpath, bearing left then right across a stile. Cross the next two fields then take a diagonal path over the one after. From here are some fabulous views of the Downs with Ditchling Beacon lying almost straight ahead. Cross a stile and field to another stile, somewhat concealed amongst trees. Jointer Copse (2) is now on the right. After the next small field and stile, turn left and left again on to a bridlepath, which can be rather muddy. At the end of the bridlepath go into East End Lane (3) on the opposite side of the road. Continue until reaching Farm Lane (4). Turn right then left, over a stile, and down a footpath. Cross a stile, bear right through a field to a footbridge and stile. This path leads into a part of Stoneywish Country Park (5) and Farm Trail. Continue past some small ponds, over a stile and turn left. Keep to the left of the field, then cross a stile, footbridge and another field. Go over the stile on the left after (not the one before) a large pond.

Walk down a lane turning right, then left by a lampost and crossing the road into Boddingtons Lane (6). Proceed along the track past various charming cottages through a squeeze gate then turn left down Lodge Hill Lane (7). The picturesque village pond, the old school, now a museum and St. Margaret's Church will be on the left. At the War Memorial turn left, past the Rectory and Wings Place. Having reached the crossroads in the village centre, turn left up the High Street (8) and turn right into East End Lane, just past Ditchling Gallery. Turn right at the sign indicating The Old Meeting House (9). This quaint twitten, a Sussex word for alley, leads back to the car park.

Points of Interest

Ditchling

As one stands at the now, all too busy crossroads of Ditchling, it is somewhat hard to imagine that less than two hundred years ago, this used to be the old coaching road to Brighton. The Bull Inn was the last stop before the horses began the long, weary climb up to Ditchling Beacon. Just up the high street, almost opposite the Bull Inn, is a rather unusual, narrow timber framed house, with a lengthy flight of external steps leading to the first floor. This was once tenements, housing many families, now beautifully restored. Behind, on substantially rising ground is St. Margaret's Church and from its porch, one has a birds eye view, across a jumble of rooftops, to the properties either side of South Street and West Street. On the furthest corner is the building that used to be home to the famous Ditchling Press, founded by Hilary Pepler. The architectural gem of Ditchling is opposite the entrance to the church. This is the impressive Tudor house, Wings Place. It is known that Henry VIII gave Anne of Cleves, his fourth wife, a large amount of land at Ditchling as part of the divorce settlement but whether she actually lived at Wings Place is questionable.

Whilst exploring Ditchling, don't miss the interesting Regency facade of black 'Mathematical Tiles' facing the house near the wagon shed on the

Ditchling High Street.

Green, by the church. Or the charming cottages of Church Lane and the lovely old Meeting House in the twitten.

Ditchling Museum

The old Victorian School by the village pond and Green, has become a museum of, amongst other things, local history. It is open throughout the year, although times vary during winter months.

Stoneywish Country Park

An interesting farm trail with all the usual farm animals, a pets corner and an area of ponds and wildlife. It is also open throughout the year with times differing in the winter.

"Do you really want me to move, I'm enjoying this hedge".

Ditchling Beacon

In days gone by, a beacon or fire, used to be lit on the summit, to warn of imminent danger. At 814 ft. high, it could be seen clearly from the coast in the south, to the North Downs. Evidence has been found suggesting occupation during the Iron Age and subsequently during Roman times. This stretch of downland is now a nature reserve and attracts many visitors, not only to enjoy the spendid views but the variety of walks that can be found in all directions.

Walk 5

ALFRISTON

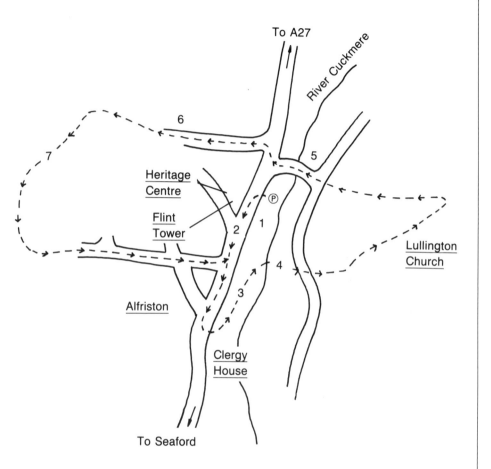

1. **Alfriston**
2. **Village Square**
3. **The Tye**
4. **White Bridge**
5. **Long Bridge**
6. **Winton Street**
7. **South Downs Way**

Walk 5

ALFRISTON

Distance	Approx. 3¾ miles. Shorter walk approx 2¼ miles.
Route	Alfriston — Village Square — The Tye — White Bridge — Long Bridge — Winton Street — South Downs Way — Alfriston.
Maps	O/S Pathfinder 1324.
Start/Parking	Alfriston is about a mile and a half from the A27 Lewes to Eastbourne road. There are two car parks at the village entrance.
Public Transport	726 Eastbourne to Seaford.
Refreshments	Alfriston has an excellent selection of pubs, restaurants and teashops.

An impressive walk that encompasses the surrounding downland to the east of Alfriston and, for a slightly longer walk, to the west as well. The village itself, mentioned in Domesday and earlier, has a picture-book setting with ancient cottages, shops and inns lining the High Street and overlooking the Tye towards the magnificent St. Andrews Church. It lies on the edge of meadows, abutting the river Cuckmere, that wends its way through the valley towards the sea at Cuckmere Haven, about four miles away. Either side are the Downs, sometimes rolling, sometimes steep, full of wild flowers, scenic walks and history.

There are stories too, about smuggling in Alfriston, ghosts that were and perhaps still are resident in some of the houses; about the people, who lived here more than a hundred years ago and the various trades that were carried out. It is not really so very different today, the trades of course have changed, the main one now being tourism, which keeps the hotels, shops and

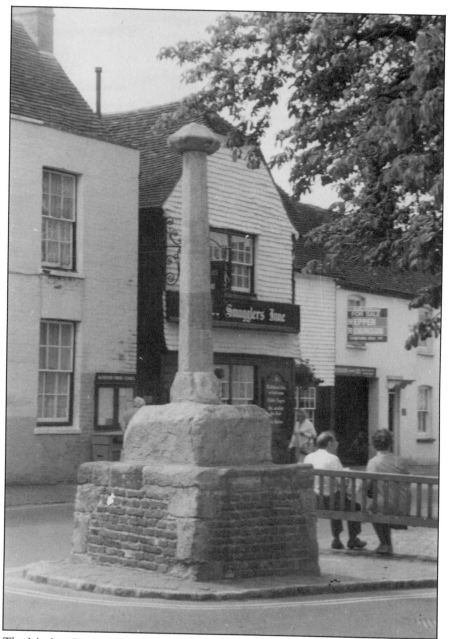

The Market Cross, Alfriston.

restaurants in business. No longer does the blacksmith wield his hammer at the anvil, the saddler stitch leather or the grocer brew beer. Instead the visitor gazes with pleasure at this incredibly pretty village, visits the museums, does some shopping, walks along the towpath and then has a cream tea. Unfortunately, at the height of summer it does get busy and traffic can be a problem. Out of season, when it is quiet, one can wander around leisurely, enjoy the atmosphere and watch the setting sun send a gold light and long shadows across the Windover Hill.

Route Directions

Go to one of the two car parks in Alfriston (1). both are opposite each other. From there, turn right at the exit from Dene car park, or left from Willows car park. Walk along the pavement until reaching the village square (2). Continue down the high street, past the Star Inn, until getting to a large Victorian property on the left. Ahead lies Denes Place Hotel. Between these two is a sign saying 'The Clergy House' and it is also the entrance to the Tye (3) or village green. Cross the Tye, keeping the church to the right, make towards a wooden fence and turn right along a tarmac footpath leading to White Bridge (4) and the River Cuckmere. Stay on the path, having crossed the bridge, until reaching a road. Go through the gate opposite, by the side of a converted barn and uphill until there is an open field on the right and a wooden sign. If you wish to visit Lullington church, keep straight on to the top of the hill. If not, turn left and take the diagonal path across the next two fields. Go over the stile and turn left down a sunken lane. At the bottom, proceed along the road, over Long Bridge (5) and at the T-junction beyond, cross the road to the footpath. For a shorter walk, turn left back to Alfriston. To explore the western downland, turn right. Turn left at the next road, this is Winton Street (6). At the top of the hill continue ahead along the chalk bridlepath and turn left at the foot of the Downs. Ascend the track which eventually bears slightly right. At the top of the Downs is a sign marking the South Downs Way (7) and at this junction turn left. From here there are extensive views eastwards, across Alfriston to Windover Hill and southwards to the sea at Cuckmere Haven. Continue along the track that will bear left and start descending. At the bottom go along the road, still going downhill, across a crossroads and on arriving at the Star Inn, turn left into Alfriston.

Points of Interest

Alfriston

This village is like an open air museum, preserved with considerable care and attention. In the centre of the village square stands the Market Cross, erected in the reign of Henry IV to ensure "all persons who traded in the weekly market, traded honestly and fairly". The enchanting Georgian bow-windowed village store, has been a grocers for more than a hundred years and the nearby Smugglers Inn is where the notorious smuggler, Stanton Collins once lived.

The Star Inn, Alfriston.

Further down the high street is the showpiece, The Star Inn and opposite The George Inn, both 14th century. Nearby, Magpie Gift Shop shows a false facade but its interior structure indicates it was an early Wealden house.

The history of the village is fairly extensive, so if you would like more detailed information, visit the Alfriston Heritage Centre, featured on page 38, or there are a few informative books on sale locally.

Alfriston Heritage Centre and Blacksmiths' Museum

A 15th century beamed forge, partially open to the roof, with two hearths, is now a blacksmith's, farrier's and wheelwright's museum. The adjoining Heritage Centre, where horses were once tied whilst waiting to be shod, contains a history of the village from Saxon times until the twentieth century. It is open from Easter until the end of October.

The Clergy House

A 14th century Priest House constructed of oak framing, filled with wattle and daub. The main hall is open to the rafters and has a rammed chalk floor. It was the first property to be purchased by the National Trust in 1896 for the sum of ten pounds. It is open to the public throughout the season.

Lullington Church

Set on the hilltop, this tiny church dates from the 13th century. However, it was originally much larger and what is now left, is in fact a part of the chancel. Services are still held once a month.

The Flint Tower

Sited in Denes Car Park, at the entrance to the village, is this rather strange conical flint tower. It was built about 1800. At the time the Duke of Wellington had his troops stationed along this coastline because of the threat of an invasion by Napoleon from France. The original use of the tower is still unknown, although there are several theories. Could it have been a shot tower, a dovecote, a kiln of some sort, a gunstore or simply the local lock-up? Perhaps one day, somebody, somewhere will be able to prove something about it.

Walk 6

RUSHLAKE GREEN AND WARBLETON

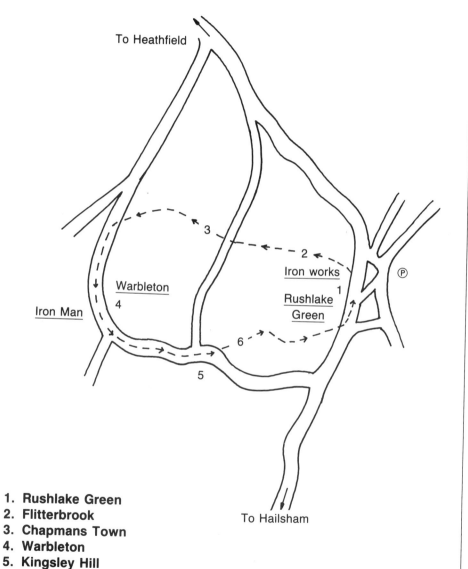

1. **Rushlake Green**
2. **Flitterbrook**
3. **Chapmans Town**
4. **Warbleton**
5. **Kingsley Hill**
6. **Toll Wood**

Walk 6

RUSHLAKE GREEN AND WARBLETON

Distance	Approx. 3 miles.
Route	Rushlake Green — Flitterbrook — Chapmans Town — Warbleton — Kinglsey Hill — Toll Wood — Rushlake Green.
Maps	O/S Pathfinder 1290.
Start/Parking	At Rushlake Green, on the Hailsham to Heathfield road.
Public Transport	Local Rider 355 and Local Rider 201 to Rushlake Green.
Refreshments	The Horse and Groom, Rushlake Green. Warbill-in-Tun Inn, Warbleton.

One of the noticeable things about many of the villages in the High Weald is their feeling of peacefulness. This is particularly so at Rushlake Green, where the green itself seems to bend over the brow of the hill and the slender iron village sign provides a pinnacle. There is no church at Rushlake Green. It lies within the parish of Warbleton, the actual church being about a mile and a half to the west.

The tree-lined pathway that descends from Rushlake Green to the footbridge, crossing the rust-coloured Flitterbrook, gives wonderful scope for the imagination. Was it perhaps, owned in the 16th century by the Iron Man, Richard Woodman? (mentioned in Points of Interest). How many men toiled in the iron mills for a pittance? Where did they live? The site of the old ironworks by the Flitterbrook, has long since been taken over by nature, thistles, ragwort and hogweed

The Twisted Tree in Toll Wood, with Jasper in the background.

grow freely and the stream now wanders idly through trees and undergrowth.

Climbing the wooded hillside to open fields, a glimpse of the substantial tower of Warbleton church comes into view. The Downs from Windover in the east to Mount Caburn and beyond, in the west can be seen on a clear day. A few partridge, suddenly disturbed, flap madly and fly from the safety of the long grass. At Warbleton the flower filled garden of Warbill-in-Tun Inn is irresistible. To linger for a while to enjoy the quiet atmosphere and for refreshment is a must, before walking back through Toll Wood. This well kept woodland trail is beautiful. There are some fine examples of trees, including the most curiously twisted tree I have ever seen. Bluebells, celandines and anenomes edge the paths in spring. In the autumn, purple blackberries, red rosehips and golden leaves provide a wealth of colour.

Route Directions

Walking northwards at Rushlake Green (1), take the signed footpath to the left, through the actual garden of a cottage, almost next door to the Horse and Groom public house. Cross the stile and go down the hill. On the left is the rather untidy site of the old Ironworks, to the right is the mellow bricked property of Marklye. Cross a stile and wooden footbridge, noticing the rusty colour of a stream named the Flitterbrook (2). Then follow the path up through woodland and across a field. From here, there is a splendid view across a wide range of the South Downs. Carry on through the next two fields until reaching a lane. Although it has only a few scattered houses, it is for some strange reason called Chapmans Town (3). Take the footpath immediately opposite, go down past a pond strewn with waterlilies, climb the slope, bear right at the next gate and cross the field, keeping to the left of the properties ahead. Now, having reached the road, turn left and follow it down into Warbleton (4), past the church and the War-Bill-in-Tun Inn.

Turn left at a T-junction and ascend Kingsley Hill (5). When just over the brow, having passed a sign pointing back to Chapmans Town, turn left along a footpath leading, first through Toll Wood (6), and then a field. The next stile goes back into woodland. Now follow the footpath, which after crossing the Flitterbrook yet again, finally leads up the hill to Rushlake Green.

Points of Interest

The Wealden Ironworks

During the 16th and 17th centuries, the scattered parish of Warbleton rang to the sounds of working iron forges and furnaces sited across the upper reaches of the Cuckmere river, where iron ore is plentiful in the sandstone. The water, correctly channelled, provided power to turn the giant wheels that operated the machinery to make iron ore into molten metal. At an iron furnace, it was then poured into moulds to make cast iron goods. At an iron forge it was hammered for wrought iron.

The Iron Man

Richard Woodman, known as the Iron Man, owned two furnaces, a forge and employed a hundred people, when still in his twenties. He was also a church warden at St. Mary's and lived in Warbleton. His refusal to accept England's return to Catholicism under the fanatical Queen Mary I, was his downfall, as his beliefs subsequently became public knowledge. He was finally arrested and imprisoned in St. Mary's church tower and in 1557, at the age of thirty, was burned at the stake in Lewes.

Warbleton

The church of St. Mary the Virgin, was mainly constructed in the 13th and 14th centuries with later additions. Some of the stained glass dates from the 15th century. Opposite, the somewhat altered Warbill-in-Tun Inn goes back to the 17th century. Its strange name, which sounds like a play on Warbleton, was supposedly acquired during the Civil War, by soldiers opening a barrel or tun of beer with a battle axe.

Rushlake Green

Rushlake Green is the most populated part of the Warbleton parish. The road to this village has ascended about four hundred feet from the Hailsham region. Around the green are a varied selection of houses and cottages, the Horse and Groom pub, the village store and Post Office, the old forge and on the northern edge, a large property called Marklye.

About a mile to the east, in a secluded position, are the remains of a fifteenth century Augustinian priory. For many years the habitable part was a farmhouse and then, latterly, became a hotel.

Rushlake Green.

The Warbill-in-Tun Inn at Warbleton.

Walk 7

FAIRLIGHT

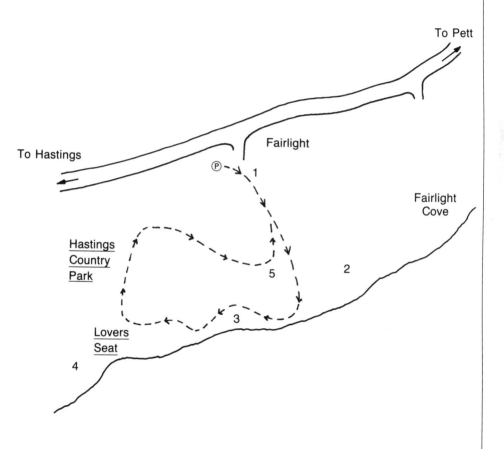

To Pett

To Hastings

Fairlight

Fairlight Cove

Hastings Country Park

Lovers Seat

1. **Fairlight**
2. **Fire Hills**
3. **Covehurst Bay**
4. **Covehurst Wood**
5. **Coastguard Cottages**

Walk 7

FAIRLIGHT

Distance	Approx. 2 miles.
Route	Fairlight — Fire Hills — Covehurst Bay — Covehurst Wood — Coastguard Cottages — Fairlight.
Maps	O/S Pathfinder 1291.
Start/Parking	At the Car Park, sited just before the church at Fairlight, on the road from Hastings.
Public Transport	44/344 Bus, Rye to Hastings. Local Rider 345.
Refreshments	The Fairlight Cove Hotel, Fairlight Cove.

This stunning walk does not really include a village in the true sense of the word, for Fairlight is merely a hamlet of strung out cottages huddled against the hillside. Its larger and not very attractive sister, Fairlight Cove, lies at the bottom of the hill, less than a mile away. However, Fairlight itself borders on to some of the most spectacular cliff top scenery, unsurpassed in East Sussex. The cliffs of reddish sandstone are somewhat unexpected in this area, in fact almost reminiscent of Dorset coastline, give way to wooded valleys running down towards the sea.

A conspicuous landmark on the skyline is St. Andrew's Church, built in 1845 in early English style, it bears a tall tower that looks more like a castellated folly. Walking down to the coastguard cottages can be chilly on this exposed tract of land, especially when the wind blows in from the east, but before turning into one of the gentle sheltered valleys, look at the panorama around you. To the east is Dungeness with the Dover cliffs beyond. To the west is the cliff line of Beachy Head and Eastbourne. On the horizon is France.

Going down to Covehurst Bay.

The Visitor Centre and cafe in the car park are open in the season, should you want more information about the area. Don't forget when walking here it can be tiring, as there is quite a lot of climbing to do, but it is well worth any extra effort that might be needed and it also shows yet another feature of the Sussex landscape.

Route Directions

From the car park at Fairlight (1) proceed down the tarmac path towards the sea. The area to the left is known as Fire Hills (2) because of the abundance of gorse. Having passed the coastguard cottages, turn right along the cliff top path, then follow the steep track downhill. From here are some beautiful views across the cliffs to Covehurst Bay (3). At various points throughout the walk are several well placed seats, so one can sit and enjoy the scenery. Having reached one of these seats, turn left down a sudden flight of steps leading into an enchanting valley with the path then crossing a tree lined brook and climbing the other side to Covehurst Wood (4). Near the top, after passing a seat, turn right along the tree lined ridge with some steps to the left and continue uphill, keeping the fence to the right. Cross a stile, turn right, cross the field and another stile behind a shack. Now proceed ahead towards the coastguard cottages (5), then keeping them to the right, go through the next two gates turning left up the bridlepath, back to the car park at Fairlight.

Points of Interest

Hastings Country Park

This country park, where the geology is unique, covers 260 hectares from Hastings to Fairlight. It is included in the High Weald area of outstanding natural beauty. A rich variety of wildlife can be seen here as the terrain varies enormously from grassland, heathland, woodland and seashore.

The Lover's Seat

One very prettily positioned seat at Fairlight is known as "Lover's Seat". Long, long ago a beautiful girl from Rye gained the affections of a naval Captain. Her parents disapproved strongly of the match and sent her to live on a remote farm just near where Lover's Seat is now placed. It was on this spot that the girl, by means of a light, was able to signal her whereabouts to the waiting Captain, who was sailing his cutter in the seas below. They declared their love for each other and married in secrecy, with the cutter's crew acting as look-outs in case of discovery. All went well and this tale has a good ending too, which is quite unusual in folklore. Apparently, a reconcilliation was effected soon after the ceremony with all concerned and the couple lived happily ever after.

Pett

This charming little village, on the hill just north of Fairlight, has a 19th century church, one or two nice inns and the pleasant and secluded beach of Pett Level at its foot.

Coastguard Cottages, Fairlight.

Coming up from Covehurst Bay.

Walk 8

WALDRON

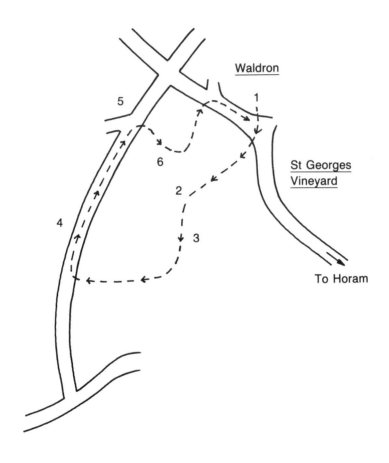

1. **Waldron**
2. **Middle Wood**
3. **The Grubs**
4. **Moat Lane**
5. **Hawkhurst Common**
6. **Middle Wood**

Walk 8

WALDRON

Distance	Approx. 2½ miles.
Route	Waldron — Middle Wood — The Grubs — Moat Lane — Hawkhurst Common — Middle Wood — Waldron.
Maps	O/S Pathfinder 1289.
Start/Parking	In the village centre by the Star Inn. Waldron lies about two and a half miles south west of the A267, near Heathfield.
Public Transport	Local Rider 258 from Heathfield.
Refreshments	The Star Inn, Waldron.

A gentle, unassuming walk, through wooded countryside and farmed fields. Certainly sheltered in most parts, which was a blessing, for when I walked here in October, although sunny, a strong wind blew heralding perhaps, a cold winter. Judging by the holly trees I saw 'en route', it will certainly be a cold winter, for they were all laden with berries.

Waldron is a very secluded village with some quaint, weather tiled cottages, a 12th century church, a village store, a vineyard and a lovely old pub. It lies south-west of Heathfield, near Possingworth Park, which is where one of the two sources of the Cuckmere River rises. A tributary of the Cuckmere meanders through the woodland in this walk and nearby, a substantial area of freshly planted oaks are growing alongside yellow gorse, bracken and hazel. There was evidence of honeysuckle and nightshade, their red berries tracing the hedgerows and here and there, under the trees, was the promise of bluebells in the spring.

To walk at Waldron on a Sunday morning, or any morning for that matter, finishing for lunch at The Star Inn, is a very appealing prospect.

The Star Inn, Waldron.

Route Directions

Go to the far corner of the churchyard, behind the church in Waldron (1). Cross the stile and the field, noting the view of the splendid Waldron House. Go through the gate and the next field keeping Middle Wood (2) to the right. Turn right after the next gateway and immediately left. Follow the edge of the field, keeping the copse to the right. Now take the footpath into woodland, strangely named The Grubs (3). Continue until reaching a wide rather muddy path, turn right, then left back into the woods. This bit is rather tricky so do note directions carefully. Cross a tiny footbridge, turn left and follow the stream. The path will move away from it when nearing the end of the woods. Now turn right. Keep to the edge of the field, then proceed diagonally across the next one and cross the stile. Staying to the right, go past the copse, to the stile beyond. Go over this and turn right into the wide leafy Moat Lane (4). Walk along here for three quarters of a mile, past an incoming lane from the left, signed to Hawkhurst

Common (5) and turn right at the next gateway. Cross the stile at the far end of the field which leads into Middle Wood (6). Take the path through the woodland and continue until reaching the second stile on the left, cross this and the field ahead that ultimately leads to a recreation area. After the gate, turn right along the road to Waldron.

Points of Interest

Waldron

The charm of this mid-Sussex village lies in its "away from it all' atmosphere and aura of peacefulness. The name Waldron is derived from the Saxon word, "Walda", meaning woody ground. The square 12th century church, set back and barely visible from the road, has one of the three Saxon fonts that remain in Sussex, although this one is not in use, but placed outside the church for everyone to see. Inside, one of the most interesting features is the beautiful lancet window decorated with a simple, corn and grape vine motif. Just south of the church grounds are several, curiously shaped soft rocks, resembling scoops of caramel, lying side by side. Opposite, is an old oast house, a reminder that hops were once grown in this part of Sussex.

St. George's Vineyard

A pretty vineyard in the centre of Waldron with some ancient buildings, including a 300 year old barn. It produces some excellent English wine and is open to visitors from April to the end of October, then at weekends until Christmas.

Walk 9

HARTFIELD AND WITHYHAM

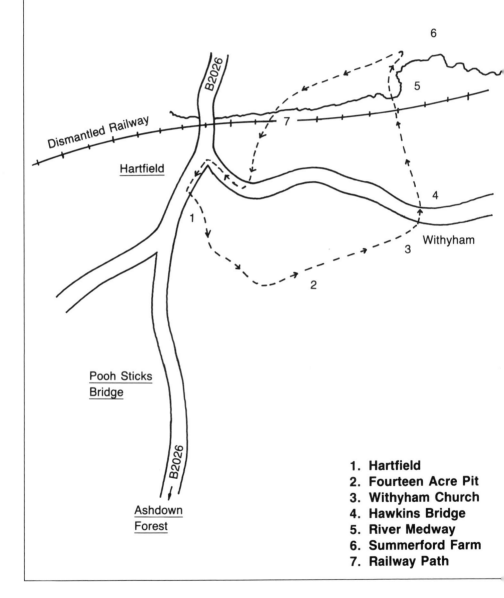

1. Hartfield
2. Fourteen Acre Pit
3. Withyham Church
4. Hawkins Bridge
5. River Medway
6. Summerford Farm
7. Railway Path

Walk 9

HARTFIELD AND WITHYHAM

Distance	Approx. 3 miles.
Route	Hartfield — Fourteen Acre Pit — Withyham Church — Hawkins Bridge — River Medway — Summerford Farm — Railway Path — Hartfield.
Maps	O/S Pathfinder 1248.
Start/Parking	In village centre, sited on the B2026, which joins the A22 near Uckfield.
Public Transport	County Rider 265. 291 Tunbridge Wells to East Grinstead.
Refreshments	The Anchor Inn and The Hay Wagon Inn at Hartfield. The Dorset Arms, Withyham.

The village of Hartfield and the ancient hamlet of Withyham are found on the fringes of Ashdown Forest, which at its highest point is over 700 feet above sea level. It is a scenically beautiful area of heathland full of alternating hues, with silver birches and conifers perched on the endless horizons.

Walking from Hartfield through very pretty undulating countryside, frost still on the ground and a clear blue sky above, one became aware of the strong silhouettes and sharpened images of winter. The recently bared trees, each branch clearly outlined, the distinctive rounded shapes of oast houses, the tall slender spire of St. Mary the Virgin at Hartfield and the square contour, tucked firmly against the hillside, of the 17th century church at Withyham. This hamlet was formerly a part of the domain of the Sackvilles, Earls of Dorset, whose seat was at Buckhurst Park, about half a mile to

Lych Gate Cottage, Hartfield.

the south. It was often known as "Sackville country" and the delightful old inn is still called "The Dorset Arms".

Beyond Withyham are the marshes and meadows surrounding the Medway river. It does seem incredible that this gently flowing stream becomes a wide river, heading for the North Sea at Sheerness. However, here red willows line the banks, bullrushes grow in clumps and a motley collection of ducks swim by, untroubled by the chilly waters. This circular route crosses the old disused railway line from Tunbridge Wells, a trail in itself, before starting to return towards Hartfield.

Route Directions

From the centre of Hartfield (1), go up a lane between the Anchor Inn and the Hay Wagon Inn, continue until reaching the church and then cross the stile opposite. Keep to the left and follow the edge of the next two fields. Cross a stile and take the left footpath through a field. Now go over another stile and follow a diagonal track across an exceptionally large field called, Fourteen Acre Pit (2). It descends into a valley with a wood and pond to the right and Withyham church (3), standing on the hill behind. Cross yet another stile and turn right along the road to Withyham. Now turn left, just before Hawkins Bridge (4). Should you want to visit Withyham itself, continue up the hill for a short distance, where the small hamlet and The Dorset Arms are clustered around the church.

Having turned left, proceed through the field to a stile, between an ugly red-roofed barn and a gate. Carry on until reaching another stile and footbridge. Go over these and also a disused railway track. Note the fine line of Red Willows on the right. Make for the bridge on the right that passes over the mere beginning of the River medway (5) and proceed across the field, along the river bank, turning left to ascend into woodland. On reaching a wide track turn left, to the right is Summerford Farm (6). Follow the bridlepath uphill then keep to the right of a field, past a copse, turn left then right and cross a footbridge and stile. You will now be on a different part of the old railway path (7). Go over the stile ahead and walk along the right side of the next two fields. Go to the dead tree in the far corner and behind, discreetly hidden, is a stile. Cross to the far side of the field beyond, then turn right along the road back into Hartfield.

Points of Interest

Hartfield

A quaint village, immortalized by the writer, A.A. Milne, who lived at the nearby, Cotchford Farm. Although the main road through Hartfield is rather busy, it does not really detract in any way from its charm and atmosphere. As at Withyham, due to the Sackville influence, there used to be a Dorset Arms, now renamed The Hay Wagon Inn. Just up the road leading to the church is the minute 16th century Lych Gate Cottage. Originally it was joined to the property next door by an arch, thus forming a wide entrance into the churchyard. Now only half remains and this was restored in 1943.

At the southern end of the High Street is Pooh Corner, the sweetshop where Christopher Robin paid a weekly visit with his nanny "Alice" to buy sweets. You can still buy sweets here, as well as souvenirs or "Pooh-phanalia" as it is called, in memory of the famous stories

Christopher Robin's Sweetshop.

written by A.A. Milne over sixty years ago, for his son Christopher Robin.

Pooh Sticks Bridge

A visit to this area isn't complete without seeing "Pooh Bridge" and perhaps even playing Pooh Sticks. Pooh car park is about two miles from Hartfield and the signed walk takes about fifteen minutes or so, through attractive, although often muddy woodland. For the Pooh enthusiasts, there is "Pooh's Forest Map" on sale at Pooh Corner. It details a seven mile walk with places of interest related to Christopher Robin, Owl, Piglet, Rabbit, and of course, Winnie-the-Pooh.

Ashdown Forest

This glorious stretch of forest and heathland sits on a high plateau in a sort of triangle formed by East Grinstead, Groombridge and Uckfield. At one time it was densely populated with trees and, until the 17th century, used as a royal hunting ground with hunting lodges placed on its perimeters. By then a good deal of deforestation had already taken place, partially due to the great Sussex ironworks needing wood to turn into charcoal for feeding the furnaces. Many large oaks were also felled and used in shipbuilding. Today it is peaceful, serene and one of the finest areas in the south for walkers, cyclists and naturalists.

The views across the ever-changing panorama are magnificent, be it early spring when the yellow gorse is in bloom, soon followed by pink heather and the soft tints of summer. Or after the rich golden colours of autumn have faded, the heathland is transformed once more by the delicate frosts of winter, dusting every tree, plant, hedgerow and spider's web with particles of white ice.

Pooh Sticks Bridge.

Jasper and Jeffrey playing Pooh Sticks at Pooh Sticks Bridge.

Walk 10

NORTHIAM AND GREAT DIXTER

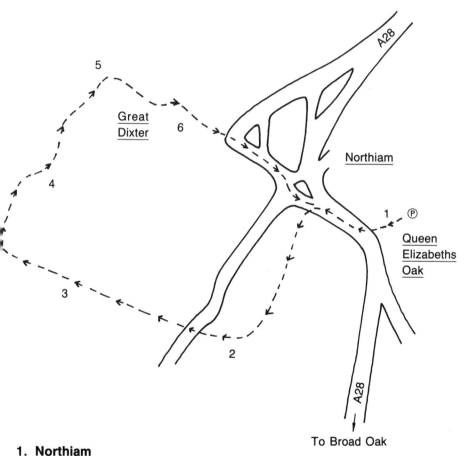

1. **Northiam**
2. **Strawberry Hole Cottages**
3. **Sussex Border Path**
4. **Four Acre Shaw**
5. **Little Dixter**
6. **Great Dixter**

Walk 10

NORTHIAM AND GREAT DIXTER

Distance   Approx. 3½ miles.

Route   Northiam — Strawberry Hole Cottages —
                      Sussex Border Path — Four Acre Shaw —
                      Little Dixter — Great Dixter — Northiam.

Maps   O/S Pathfinder 1271.

Start/Parking   In Northiam car park, by the church on the A28,
                      the Broad Oak to Tenterden road.

Public Transport Local Rider 348 and 300.
                      400/401 from Hastings.

Refreshments   The Crown and Thistle, Northiam.
                      The Six Bells, Northiam.

I know Sussex so well, yet I am still suprised by the tremendous variety
in both the landscape and architecture that can happen after only a short
journey. This was so at Northiam, lying just a few miles from the River
Rother that marks the Kent boundary. In the distance, on a clear day, are
glimpses of the flat, secretive Romney Marsh and to the south lies the coast
and the historic Cinque Ports town of Rye, the remaining vista is hilly and
wooded.

Northiam and the 15th century hall house, Great Dixter are in fact very
close but this horseshoe, looped walk that joins them, should not be missed.
The path travels through undulating landscape that offers some of the
loveliest scenery on the Sussex, Kent borders. It passes through meadows,
over streams, by woodland and into open fields. When I walked here, in
the autumn, the trees were heavy with red and gold leaves and the many
pheasants, richly coloured, squawked at the unwelcome intrusion of my

Boxer dog, Jasper, before flying clumsily away from the stubble of the cornfields. As we rambled up the hill towards the oast houses of Dixter, the hedgerows were laced with "old man's beard" and sheep grazed disinterestedly around us. At Dixter the footpath merges with the road to wind gently back into the village of Northiam.

Here, it is interesting to notice how the type of house has changed, from the flint and brick downland cottage, to the often large, fully timbered property, built in true Kentish style.

Route Directions

On leaving the car park on the A28, by the church, cross the road and turn right, taking the footpath by the side of the old post office in the centre of Northiam (1). Cross the recreation ground, keeping the hedge to the right. Go through a field, cross a stile and the next field, noting the oast house of Strawberry Hole Cottages (2) on the left. Go over the stile in the far right corner and follow the path ahead. Cross the road and stile opposite, then into a field, keeping the woods to the left. Here, the very beautiful hilly countryside is interspersed with woodland, fields and streams, and not a house in sight. The track now being taken along the valley is a part of the Sussex Border Path (3). Go through the next gate and stile on the left, then turn right. Go over a stile and footbridge. Proceed through a field and copse, into another field, keeping the hedge and stream to the right. After about a third of the way, cross a fairly well hidden footbridge. Continue up the hill. The surrounding fields are known as Four Acre Shaw (4). Go over a stile and here the rooftops of Little Dixter (5) come into view. Keeping the hedges to the right, continue to the next stile by a small pond. Proceed through the field beyond, behind the oast houses and having reached a tarmac path turn right, through the gateway. Follow the path, past the lovely 15th century Great Dixter Manor (6), continuing along the road bearing right, back into Northiam.

Points of Interest

Northiam

Few villages can have such a wealth and variety of timbered houses, originating from different periods, as Northiam. One of the most unusual, is a large weather-boarded property on three floors and dating from the late eighteenth century. It overlooks the small tree-lined common, the Queen's Oak, the memorial and the Pump House. Behind it, is a Georgian residence and St Mary's Church, the tower being Norman. The tall spire was added in the sixteenth century, then extended a further ten feet, for some reason, during the Victorian era. Next door is Church House with a handsome William and Mary frontage. To the south lies the Elizabethan mansion of Brickwall, home to the Frewens, the great family of Northiam for many generations. Now it is a school, however part of it is open to the public on certain days throughout the season.

This old Sussex saying I think, sums up the village in just two lines:-

> *Oh rare Northiam, dost far exceed*
> *Beckley, Peasmarsh, Udimore and Brede.*

The Old Village Pump, Northiam.

Queen Elizabeth's Oak

The remains of this massive oak tree, kept together by chains, is the one Queen Elizabeth I chose to sit beneath and rest on her journey to Rye on August 11th 1573. She was served a meal under its spreading

Queen Elizabeth's Oak, Northiam

branches, brought from a nearby house. She then changed her shoes, leaving the green damask pair behind, as a memento of her visit. They are still in existence and are apparently on display at Brickwall House.

Great Dixter

Today Great Dixter is probably the finest surviving example of a 15th century Hall House. Who would believe that when it was purchased in 1910 by Mr. Nathaniel Lloyd, there were two adjacent, but separate hall houses, Benenden and Dixter, lying in a derelict state, in an equally derelict farmyard.

Great Dixter.

Mr. Lloyd retained the designer, Sir Edwin Lutyens to restore both houses and construct a further wing, thus joining them and making one large manor house, but still retaining all the original features and timbers. The main hall is huge. It measures 41 feet by 26 feet and is 31 foot high. The timbers, which came from the local Wealden forests are massive. They had to be, for once they supported a Horsham stone roof and central fireplace. The beautiful landscaped gardens were also designed by Lutyens and the estate is open to the public from April to October.

Walk 11

BERWICK AND ALCISTON

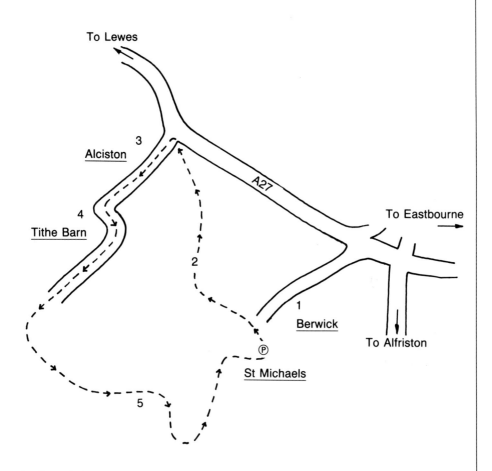

1. **Berwick**
2. **The Meadows**
3. **Alciston**
4. **Tithe Barn**
5. **New Barn**

Walk 11

BERWICK AND ALCISTON

Distance	Approx. 2½ miles.
Route	Berwick — The Meadows — Alciston — Tithe Barn — New Barn — Berwick.
Maps	O/S Pathfinder 1308.
Start/Parking	By the church at the southern end of Berwick village which is just off the A27 Lewes to Eastbourne road.
Public Transport	Cuckmere Valley Community Bus to Berwick only.
Refreshments	Cricketers Arms, Berwick. Rose Cottage, Alciston.

Neither Berwick nor Alciston are as large, as well known or as busy as, their neighbour, Alfriston. Yet, they are nevertheless beautiful in a timeless and unobtrusive way, nestling comfortably at the foot of one of the loveliest stretches of downland, offering many varied paths for the walker. The initial walk from Berwick to Alciston leads through farmed fields that have always been known to me as The Meadows. This was, presumably, because they provided lush green grazing ground and had an assortment of wild flowers gracing the hedgerows.

Alciston itself has an almost medieval atmosphere about it, especially in the mellow area of the church, Court Farm and the old Tithe Barn where hens, ducks and geese roam freely. An enchanting black pig adds to the scenery by peering nosily through a wooden fence, while sheep, cows, calves and horses wander in the nearby fields.

An amusing incident, which I must relate, happened when doing this walk. I decided to take another look at Alciston church to refresh my memory on a few details. However, to get to the church, one has to walk through a few feet of grazing land in front of Alciston Court Farm, undo the chain on the church gate, lift the latch and climb the steps. This I did, carefully shutting the gate and dropping the latch behind me. The chain I would do on the way out. After a minute, I hear a noise and turned round. Quick as a flash the friendly grey horse that I'd been chatting to earlier, had flipped the latch, climbed the steps and was leading two of his mates to the tasty pastures of the graveyard. An hour later, with the help of some residents and the banging of saucepan lids, apparently kept for this frequent occurrence, the graveyard interlopers were persuaded to go back reluctantly, to their own pastures.

To Alciston Church, but remember to shut the gates.

The return walk from Alciston follows a part of the old turnpike road that ran between Lewes and Eastbourne until 1812. Ahead lies the magnificent Windover Hill, which is more than 700 feet above sea level. On the left side of Windover, (not visible from here), is the huge, carved chalk figure, known as The Long Man. Berwick is a rambling village. At the southern end, built on rising ground, is the very, very lovely church, with its famous wall paintings by the Bloomsbury artists, Vanessa Bell, Quentin Bell and Duncan Grant.

Route Directions

From the small car park at Berwick (1), turn right down the lane, then turn left. Carry straight on, keeping the farm buildings and cottages to the right. Pass through a wide gateway and along the left edge of a field. From here there are spendid views of the Downs finishing at Firle Beacon. Now cross a stile, another field and a footbridge. Take a diagonal path across the meadow (2) to a further stile. Continue through the next two meadows, which are small and therefore the stiles are easily visible and then climb the hill.

On reaching the top of the hill, keep to the left of the converted barn. Between the two adjacent cottages is the pathway into Alciston (3). It is both hidden and somewhat overgrown, so you need to look for it carefully. After this, turn left into the village. The long lane winds past brick and flint cottages, pretty gardens, the Rose Cottage Inn, Alciston Church and Alciston Court Farm. Finally, it turns sharp left and there is the magnificent Tithe Barn (4). Follow the lane as it bends to the right, then as it reaches the Downs and becomes a bridleway, turn left. Carry on eastwards along this track that once was the site of the old Turnpike Road.

Having passed, on the right, a collection of barns, inappropriately called New Barn (5), bear left. Go up the incline and turn right then left, along a narrow path. This leads to Berwick Church, back to the car park and Berwick Village.

Points of Interest

Berwick

To the left, on entering the village, is the Tye or 'Common Ground'. On one side of this is a pond, fringed with farm buildings, on the other are various mounds and ditches thought to be indications of an earlier Berwick, possibly of the Saxon era, so predominant in this part of Sussex. Opposite, the delightful Cricketers Arms offers attractive gardens, sheltered tables and good pub food. The assorted houses and cottages, some dating from Elizabethan times, are beautifully kept and it is worth noting the variety of materials used in their construction.

At the end of the village, next to the car park, is the recently erected parsonage, whilst ahead is the splendid Victorian rectory, now a private residence. This was rebuilt during the time of Rev. Boys Ellman, Curate of Berwick from 1837 to 1843 and Rector from 1846 to 1906. He died at the age of 91 and his grave is in the churchyard.

St. Michaels and All Angels

There has been a church at Berwick for certainly over a thousand years. The present one was erected during the 12th century. But like so many rural churches by the time the Victorian era arrived, it had fallen into a very sad state of disrepair. It was not until the Rev. Boys Ellman became Rector in the latter half of the nineteenth century, that a complete restoration was carried out.

It is unusual to find clear glass windows in a church but this is so at Berwick. The original leaded windows were destroyed during the war and the Bishop felt that clear glass, apart from making it lighter and brighter would also offer an excellent opportunity to introduce wall paintings. Having finally obtained permission, to install the murals, and this was after some considerable difficulties with the Parish Church Council, agreement was then needed from the Bloomsbury artists, Vanessa Bell, Quentin Bell and Duncan Grant to undertake the work. This was reached on the basis that the murals could be painted on plasterboard in their studio at the nearby Charleston Farmhouse where they lived. They would then be secured to the church walls. Work was completed by December 1942. It was then hung and dedicated by the Bishop in 1943.

The imaginative wall paintings, depicting various scenes, some using the Downs as a backcloth, add a most unusual aspect to this charming church, where the Sussex landscape is clearly visible through plain glass windows.

Alciston

Alciston, like Berwick, has no shops and consists of a rambling lane, ultimately leading to the Downs, with various properties bordering onto it. One of them is the Rose Cottage Inn, dating from the seventeenth century and having a curious car park lined with old advertising signs from the twenties, thirties and forties. Further on is a truly "Alice in Wonderland" cottage, seeming smaller than most and complete with a thatched roof, tumbling roses and a well in the front garden. Beyond lies the little flint walled church, parts of which are Norman. The nearby Alciston Court Farm has adjoining barns, outbuildings, farmyard and pond. It looks as though little has changed over the last few centuries. At one time the original village dwellings were clustered around the farm, but the Black Death wiped out all but a few of the inhabitants, leaving their humble homes to fall into ruin.

Tithe Barn

The massive oak beamed Tithe Barn, by Alciston Court Farm, is one of the largest in the country and still very much in use for farming purposes. Originally, Tithe Barns were built to store one tenth of annual produce, claimed by priests from their local farmers. This was the 'rent' in lieu of money. Judging by the size of tithe barns, particularly this one, the clergy must have been very comfortable indeed.

South view of the Tithe Barn.

Walk 12

SOUTHEASE AND RODMELL

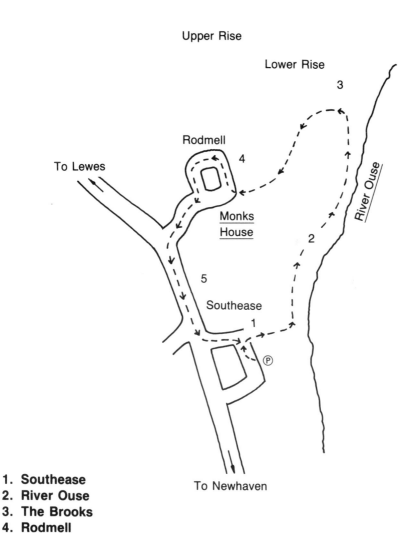

Upper Rise

Lower Rise

3

Rodmell

4

To Lewes

River Ouse

Monks House

2

5

Southease

1

P

To Newhaven

1. **Southease**
2. **River Ouse**
3. **The Brooks**
4. **Rodmell**
5. **South Downs Way**

Walk 12

SOUTHEASE AND RODMELL

Distance	Approx. 3 miles.
Route	Southease — River Ouse — The Brooks — Rodmell — South Downs Way — Southease.
Maps	O/S Pathfinder 1308.
Start/Parking	By the church in Southease, just off the A275, Lewes to Newhaven road.
Public Transport	County Rider 123, Lewes to Peacehaven.
Refreshments	The Abergavenny Arms, Rodmell.

The secluded and peaceful hamlet of Southease sits just above the River Ouse, its cluster of old houses, some half hidden by thatch, ivy, honeysuckle and clematis, are mainly centred around the tiny Norman church and a sloping stretch of Green. The church has an unusual rounded tower, one of three in Sussex, the others being at Piddinghoe and Lewes. There is a transitional chancel arch and the remains of once vivid 13th century wall paintings. When walking through this sleepy hamlet down to the River Ouse, it really does seem as though time has passed it by, unlike the neighbouring Rodmell, which is just as lovely, but in an entirely different way. Here the houses, mostly built of flint, are tastefully restored, the huge barns converted and the gardens immaculately kept.

As you wander along the Ouse valley, where marsh marigolds grow in profusion and only an expert could identify the different bird cries, look towards Itford Hill on the far side of the river. Some years ago a Bronze Age settlement was discovered on its slopes and it is now rated as a key British archaeological site.

It has to be impossible not to linger on the river banks enjoying the wildlife, flowers and views or simply watching the tidal river meander towards Newhaven, a busy channel port dating from the late 16th century. In the opposite direction is the ancient county town of Lewes, topped by a partially ruined Norman castle and to the right is a stretch of downland culminating at Mount Caburn, a ridged hilltop that used to be an Iron Age hill fort. Looking northwards, in the middle of the Ouse marshes, are two small hills called Lower Rise and Upper Rise. The curious legend about these two mounds indicates they were gigantic shovels of earth, dug by a superhuman being, from Devil's Dyke, near Brighton. Sussex really does have the most wonderful tales and folklore.

Southease Church.

Route Directions

With the church at Southease (1) behind you, continue eastwards down the road, towards Itford Hill on the opposite side of the valley. Turn left through a squeeze gate, just before the old swing bridge and walk along the banks of the River Ouse (2). There are some fabulous views at this point. Mount Caburn and Lewes lie to the north and down river is the intriguing dockland of Newhaven. Proceed along the river bank for about a mile crossing four stiles. The large area of marshland that stretches up to Lewes ahead, is known as The Brooks (3). Having crossed the fourth stile, turn left down the river bank, through a gate and follow the gritted bridle-path, westward. Carry on along this marshland track until reaching the road leading into Rodmell (4). Turn right, bear left and left again. Directly opposite, in front of the church, is Monk's House, the home of Virginia and Leonard Woolf. Turn right past the immaculately kept flint and brick cottages, then left at The Abergavenny Arms. Take the footpath that follows the road and is, in fact, part of The South Downs Way (5). The next turning left leads back into Southease.

Points of Interest

The River Ouse

One of the major rivers of Sussex, rising in the high Wealden forests, the Ouse then sweeps down to its mouth at Newhaven. Formerly, it ran parallel to the coast entering the sea at Seaford, but during a violent storm in the 16th century, it burst through the banks at Newhaven.

Swans on the Ouse.

Probably all the low lying land from Seaford to Lewes was once a vast tidal estuary. Even a few hundred years ago, the river was considerably wider and villages such as Rodmell and Southease were almost literally on the river banks. It was navigable just beyond Lewes and horse drawn barges were a common sight. It was also ideal for that famous Sussex trade, smuggling. Records suggest that in Domesday, when Southease was owned by an Abbey near Winchester, 38,500 herring used to be paid in annual rent. I wonder; did this mean there was a fishing fleet moored here?

Monk's House, Rodmell

This converted farmhouse used to be the home of that famous Bloomsbury couple, Virginia and Leonard Woolf. Their furniture and personal items have been preserved and the interior is much as it was when they were in occupation. Tragically, Virginia Woolf committed suicide by drowning herself in the nearby River Ouse. The entire property is now owned by the National Trust and is open to visitors during the season.

Walk 13

MAYFIELD

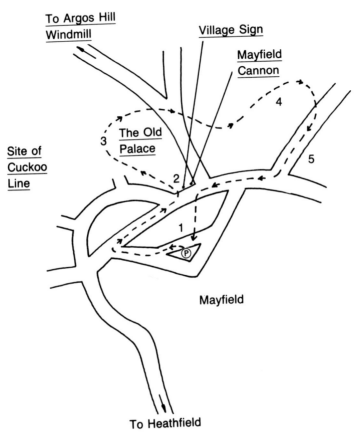

To Argos Hill Windmill

Village Sign

Mayfield Cannon

The Old Palace

Site of Cuckoo Line

Mayfield

To Heathfield

1. **Mayfield**
2. **North Street**
3. **The Old Palace**
4. **Herons Folly**
5. **Fletching Street**

Walk 13

MAYFIELD

Distance	Approx. 1¾ miles.
Route	Mayfield — North Street — The Old Palace — Heron's Folly — Fletching Street — Mayfield.
Maps	O/S Pathfinder 1269.
Start/Parking	At the Cark Park in the centre of the village, behind Middle House Hotel.
Public Transport	Local Rider 226 and 227, Mayfield to Crowborough.
Refreshments	The Rose and Crown, The Carpenters Arms and Middle House Hotel, all in Mayfield.

The picturesque village of Mayfield, once an early ironworking centre, sits squarely on a hill, with St. Dunstan's Church and Convent lording gracefully above it, their contours providing a prominent landmark for miles around.

The sloping medieval street is rich with timbered or stone buildings, including Middle House, one of the finest Elizabethan inns in England. Much of the stone used in constructing houses came from the Old Palace ruins, now incorporated in the convent. St. Dunstan's Church has a 12th century tower, the rest dating from that era, perished in the fire of 1389, which destroyed much of Mayfield as well. Rebuilding began soon after this disaster occured and it is interesting to learn that many of the present properties have much older foundations.

There is rather a quaint Sussex legend relating to St. Dunstan, the Saxon saint of Mayfield, who traded as a blacksmith. I'm sure, like all legends, it must have grown with the telling. It goes like this:- "One day St. Dunstan was hard at work in his smithy, when a very desirable woman appeared

Middle House Hotel, Mayfield.

The Rose and Crown in Fletching Street, Mayfield.

at his forge and tried to tempt him. How fortunate it was that St. Dunstan suddenly espied a cloven hoof instead of a shapely leg beneath the dress, so this was the devil in disguise. In one swoop, St. Dunstan grabbed his hot tongs and pinched the devils nose. In agony, the devil, leapt in the air and landed at the springs where the spas of Tunbridge Wells now stand, simultaneously thrusting his injured nose into the cooling waters. The tongs that were supposedly used for this memorable occasion are on display in The Old Palace.

As one rambles around the boundaries of Mayfield, on this high ridge of land, don't forget to notice the wonderful views across the Weald to both the north and south Downs.

Route Directions

On leaving the car park at Mayfield (1), turn left, down the lane and past some attractive cottages. Follow the road round, then turn right up the High Street. Between two shops and just before the church, is a narrow passage, somewhat oddly called North Street (2). Go left and follow the path which travels downhill and becomes a grassy track. Cross the stile and turn right. From here are some excellent views of the Old Palace (3). Walk over the school playing fields to a stile in the far corner, keeping the pond to the right. Turn right along the road then first left down a bridlepath. Keep to the left and in a small wooded area is a stile. Cross this and go right. Heron's Folly (4), a large manor house, is in the adjoining copse. Go over the stile ahead and bear right down a wide track. Having reached a road turn right and you will soon pass, or maybe stop at, the delightful Rose and Crown Inn. Take the right hand fork and proceed up Fletching Street (5) past The Carpenter's Arms into the village centre, turning left by the Middle House Hotel to the car park.

Points of Interest

The Old Palace

The 14th century remains of the Old Palace are skillfully interwoven with the more recent structure of the convent. The slender arches standing out proudly from their comparatively modern backcloth.

It is suggested that the original palace and church would have been wooden. As they were constructed during Saxon times, when wood was the common material for building, this is certainly more than likely. The

The Village Sign.

palace has had many landlords, witnessed many royal visits and has seen many changes to its structure over the years. The most dramatic being in 1740, when the Great Hall was unroofed and the stone slabs were used in constructing houses in the village. The convent was established in 1872 and the Great Hall, now the chapel, is open for visitors, but you do need to telephone the convent beforehand to make an appointment.

The Village Sign

A lovely and unusual village sign indicating the name Mayfield, could be a play on the words "Maids Fields" St. Dunstan and the devil also feature. The inscription below reads: "Following a speech by HRH The Duke of York at the Royal Academy in 1920, on the revival of village signs, The Daily Mail organised a village signs competition offering a total of £2,200 in prizes. Ten awards were made and the design from which this sign was constructed secured the second prize of £500."

The Mayfield Cannon

This 17th century cannon was discovered in one of the cinder beds of the Mayfield furnace in 1824. It remained in the Old Palace for a number of years and has only recently been put in its present position in the High Street, near the gatehouse of the convent.

Argos Hill Windmill

A fine example of an old Post Mill sited on Argos Hill, a mile or so north-west of Mayfield. It was built about 1835 and continued to be worked until 1927. Those who wish to visit, must first obtain permission from Wealden District Council.

The Cuckoo Line

The Cuckoo Line, a railway that ran between Polegate and Eridge, acquired its name from the Sussex tradition of releasing a cuckoo every spring from Heathfield Fair. It was operational by 1880 and passed through the Wealden countryside and villages of Hellingly, Horam, Heathfield, Mayfield and Rotherfield. Unfortunately, it was a victim of the 1960s closures. Now the stretch of railway track that ran by Mayfield station has been incorporated in the much needed by-pass.

Argos Hill Windmill.

Walk 14

SEDLESCOMBE

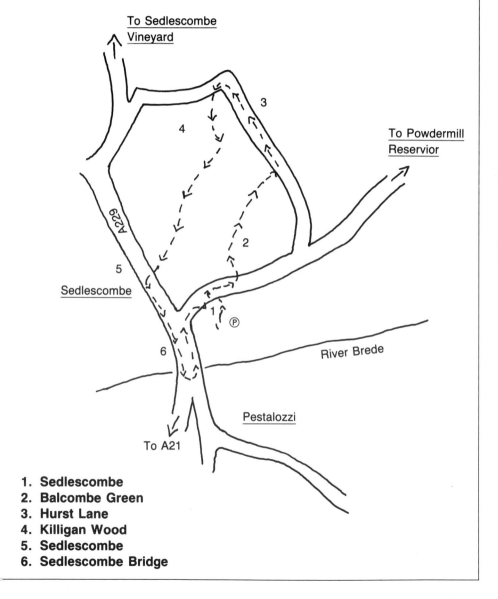

1. **Sedlescombe**
2. **Balcombe Green**
3. **Hurst Lane**
4. **Killigan Wood**
5. **Sedlescombe**
6. **Sedlescombe Bridge**

Walk 14

SEDLESCOMBE

Distance	Approx. 2½ miles.
Route	Sedlescombe — Balcombe Green — Hurst Lane — Killigan Wood — Sedlescombe — Sedlescombe Bridge.
Maps	O/S Pathfinder 1290.
Start/Parking	Sedlescombe is about a mile from the A21 Battle to Hastings road. The car park is situated just behind the village green.
Public Transport	County Rider 351. Local Rider 349, 49 and 326.
Refreshments	The Queens Head, Sedlescombe. Brickwall Hotel, Sedlescombe.

Built on a hill by the River Brede, Sedlescombe is often referred to as one of the prettiest villages in Sussex. The surrounding countryside is exceptionally lovely.

The walk travels into the woodland above Sedlescombe, past a backwater or two, down to the river, then returns through the village again. Shuffling happily along amongst the fallen leaves in Hurst Lane, the November sun filtering between the trees, I was reminded of a similar occasion when I was a child. Naturally, I was severely reprimanded for shuffling and scuffing new boots. Today, as I kicked the leaves in the air, watched their colours change in the sunlight, then as they fell, Jasper leaping on his hind legs to catch them, I reflected on the simple pleasures of being an adult.

The curious name Powdermill seems to occur frequently here. It is apparently related to the number of gundpowder mills that operated in and around Battle after the decline of the iron industry. Sometimes mills that used to grind corn changed to gunpowder. Probably it was more profitable. It is difficult to imagine this tranquil little village being at the heart of a busy industrial area. Its location on the banks of the Brede, which was much wider then, provided a useful means of transportation. The waiting barges would take iron, then subsequently gunpowder, down to Rye, where it was shipped to London. Now the river Brede is barely more than a stream and the only sign of activity is the rather too frequent traffic that crosses the bridge over it.

Sedlescombe Village.

Route Directions

Turn right from the car park in Sedlescombe (1). Almost immediately take the signed footpath on the left, just past some cottages. Go up the hill, along a short road and then through the gate ahead. Continue across the field to a stile. The area to the right, is Balcombe Green (2). Cross the stile and the next field diagonally to the furthest corner. When I walked here, there was no sign of the diagonal public footpath across the field, so I followed the perimeter. Now go over the stile, into woodland, across a footbridge and a further stile, then proceed up the hill, the surrounding countryside is now fairly densely wooded. Keeping the cottage to the left, cross the stile leading into Hurst Lane (3) and turn left.

On the right is Hurst Wood, which borders the scenic area of Powdermill Reservoir. Continue along the lane until reaching a left hand bend. Turn sharp left here onto a signed footpath leading along the edge of Killigan Wood (4) and behind some cottages. Turn right at a wide lane that becomes more of a bridlepath and bears to the left. Note Sedlescombe church on the right. Carry on until reaching a gate, go through the field ahead, cross the stile, then go down the lane, this will bear to the right. Turn left along the main road back into Sedlescombe (5). Now proceed through the village, past the village green and down to Sedlescombe Bridge (6). If you want to extend this walk there are some very pretty footpaths, either side of the bridge, along the banks of the River Brede. Now return up the hill, keeping to the right of the green and turning right just past the Queen's Head pub, back to the car park.

Points of Interest

Sedlescombe

A picturesque village clustered around a south-facing green, with a central leaden pump and rather a fine pillared shelter built over it. Plenty of interesting buildings, some more than 500 years old, to see and a few small shops to browse in.

Powdermill Reservoir

As its name suggests, this reservoir is set in the beautiful valley that, until 1825 had mills producing gunpowder. It was flooded about a hundred years later to provide water for Hastings. There are several footpaths in the surrounding woodland which, in turn, is home to a number of grey squirrels. The reservoir itself is stocked with trout for the keen angler to enjoy and a variety of bird life can be seen skimming the surface or nesting in the trees and hedgerows.

Pestalozzi

Pestalozzi children's village trust, which has an open day once a year, offers a home for children from the third world whilst being educated in this country. Once they have acquired the necessary knowledge, they return to their homeland to pass on their skills. Pestalozzi lies on the southern side of the River Brede at Oakalnds, once the home of the famous nineteenth century watercolour artist, with a strange double surname, Hercules Brabazon Brabazon.

Sedlescombe Organic Vineyard

A pretty vineyard, set in a valley on the B2244 about one mile north of Sedlescombe. It offers not only wine tasting at the wine centre but nature trails through the vineyards and woods.

A Tudor Cottage in Sedlescombe.

Walk 15

AROUND FLETCHING

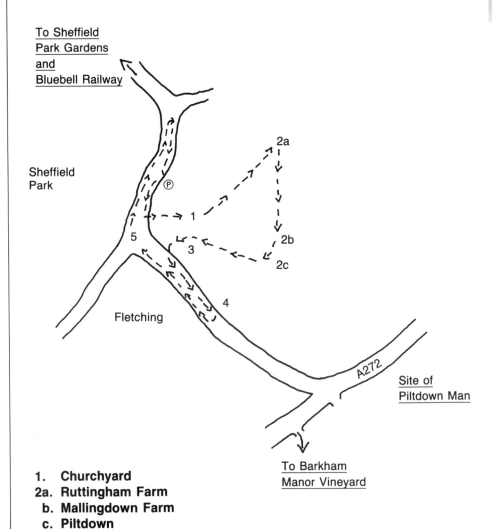

1. **Churchyard**
2a. **Ruttingham Farm**
 b. **Mallingdown Farm**
 c. **Piltdown**
3. **The Church**
4. **Water Pump**
5. **High Street**

Walk 15

AROUND FLETCHING

Distance	Approx. 1 mile.
Route	Churchyard — Footpaths to a) Ruttingham Farm or b) Mallingdown Farm or c) Piltdown — The Church — Water Pump — High Street.
Maps	O/S Pathfinder 1269.
Start/Parking	Fletching village. One mile off the A272 Newick to Maresfield.
Public Transport	County Rider 246 from Uckfield. 781/281 Eastbourne to Haywards Heath.
Refreshments	The Griffin Inn and The Rose and Crown, both in Fletching.

Fletching has to be one of the loveliest mid-Sussex Wealden villages, well preserved yet totally unspoilt.

The majority of the properties are timber framed, although some bear a Georgian frontage and there is a wonderful selection of pots and hanging baskets full of geraniums, adorning doorways and corners.

At the southern end is a fine 13 century church, with a larger than average churchyard, where some of the inscriptions on the old headstones make fascinating reading. It has two good inns, both with small car parks and attractive gardens, a village shop and Post Office and a tiny butchers. There are no gift shops, tearooms or coach parks, but in spite of that, one wonders why this lovely village with a long history, is not packed with visitors. Could it be that it is overshadowed by its much-publicized neighbours, Sheffield Park and The Bluebell Railway?

Fletching lies in the middle of rolling countryside, with several farms on its outskirts. It offers a variety of walks, and is central to four attractions, not much more than ten minutes away by car and mentioned in Points of Interest.

Its history can be traced back to Saxon times, when it must have been one of the deepest Wealden settlements. In 1264, Simon de Montfort and his army camped on the perimeter, prior to fighting and winning the Battle of Lewes against Henry III. There is a legend suggesting that the knights of Simon de Monfort who were killed in battle, were carried back to Fletching and buried beneath the nave of the church. Here too, lies Edward Gibbon, author of "The Decline and Fall of The Roman Empire". He was a great friend of the first Earl of Sheffield and when he died in 1794, he was buried in the Sheffield Mausoleum. The castellated gateway near the church is a private entrance to Sheffield Park.

Approaching the village from the A272, is a small and unusual wooden structure. This houses the old water pump and was restored in 1973.

Route Directions

This is essentially just a village ramble, with indications where the footpaths lie, if wanting to explore the undulating surrounding countryside. The easy footpaths, however, are not circular, unless one is prepared to do some main road walking, which apart from being unsafe, is also noisy.

This short walk around the village, starts to the right of the beamed cottages behind the church and passes through the pleasing well laid out churchyard (1) with flowers and yew trees. Now cross a further garden area (also belonging to the church) to the iron kissing gate. Go to the far left corner of the next field, where the track continues to Ruttingham Farm (2a) just over a mile away. Remaining in the same field and keeping the hedge to the left, cross to the other corner, where the track divides, first for Mallingdown Farm (2b), one mile, then for Piltdown (2c), one mile. Now return and visit the lovely church (3) leaving by the front gate, Cross the road and turn left. Opposite will be the old Water Pump (4). Turn back towards the village noticing the handsome Georgian fronted farmhouse next to the church and the entrance to Sheffield Park ahead. Turn right to the ancient High Street (5). At the end, just before reaching Atheralls Farm, is a footpath on the left, to Splaynes Green Farm which is just over half a mile.

The Gatehouse to Sheffield Park.

Fletching High Street.

Points of Interest

Sheffield Park

Sheffield Park Gardens covers a hundred acres. It was landscaped in the 18th century with waterfalls, lakes, rhodedendrons, azaleas, rare trees and shrubs. It is owned by The National Trust and is particularly spectacular in the spring.

Bluebell Railway

A journey into the past by steam train from Sheffield Park Station to the temporary terminus at New Coombe Bridge. Plans are afoot to take the line as far as East Grinstead.

Piltdown Man

In 1911 an amateur archaeologist, named Charles Dawson claimed to have found the fossilized remains of, as he became known as "The Piltdown Man". This was claimed to be the link in man's evolution from apes. However, in 1949, a Dr Oakley applied the fluorine dating test to the fragments and it was descovered to be a hoax. Chemical and physical evidence indicates The Piltdown Man dates from somewhere between AD1000 and 1900. The hoaxer remains unknown.

Barkham Manor Vineyard

Barkham Manor, mentioned in the Domesday and given to Earl Godwin by King Edward, was valued, prior to 1066, for the grand sum of twenty shillings. A huge thatched barn built in 1750 has recently been restored and dominates the surrounding grounds. The vineyard itself is fairly young. Planted in 1985, it is now successfully producing a variety of wines and is open to visitors.

POINTS TO REMEMBER

1) Keep to public rights of way.

2) Fasten all gates.

3) Keep dogs under control.

4) Do not leave litter around.

5) Do not disturb cattle, sheep or other animals.

6) Do not pick wild flowers.

7) Leave the countryside as you find it so others can enjoy it too.

TRANSPORT AND INFORMATION

British Rail: Train times and fares — Tel (0273) 206755

Bus Services: Bus Helpline — Tel (0273) 478007

Tourist Information Centres

Battle
88 High Street
Tel (0424) 773721

Hove
Town Hall, Norton Road
Tel (0273) 778087

Bexhill
De La Warr Pavilion
Tel (0424) 212023

Lewes
32 High Street
Tel (0273) 483448

Boship
Lower Dicker
Tel (0323) 442667

Peacehaven
Meridian Centre
Tel (0273) 582668

Brighton
10 Bartholomew Square
Tel (0273) 323775

Pevensey
Castle Cottage (Easter - Oct)
Tel (0323) 761444

Eastbourne
Cornfield Road
Tel (0323) 411400

Rye
Heritage Centre, Strand Quay
Tel (0797) 226696

Hailsham
The Library, Western Road
Tel (0323) 840604

Seaford
Station Approach
Tel (0323) 897426

Hastings
4 Robertson Terrace
Tel (0424) 718888